372.13028
L553m

W9-AUV-145

3874 03300679 3

99 WAYS

TO GET YOUR KIDS
TO DO THEIR
HOMEWORK

(AND NOT HATE IT)

CHASE BRANCH LIBRARY
17731 W. SEVEN MILE
DETROIT, MICH. 48235

CH

Also by MARY LEONHARDT

Parents Who Love Reading, Kids Who Don't

Keeping Kids Reading

99 Ways to Get Kids to Love Reading

99 Ways to Get Kids to Love Writing

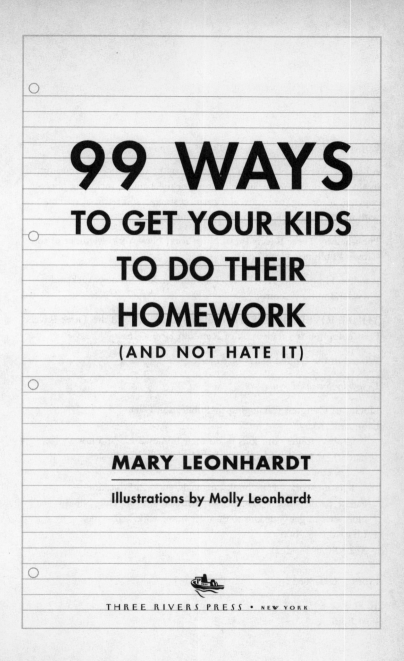

99 WAYS

TO GET YOUR KIDS
TO DO THEIR
HOMEWORK

(AND NOT HATE IT)

MARY LEONHARDT

Illustrations by Molly Leonhardt

THREE RIVERS PRESS • NEW YORK

Copyright © 2000 by Mary Leonhardt

All rights reserved. No part of this book may be reproduced or transmitted in any form or by any means, electronic or mechanical, including photo-copying, recording, or by any information storage and retrieval system, without permission in writing from the publisher.

Published by Three Rivers Press, New York, New York. Member of the Crown Publishing Group.

Random House, Inc. New York, Toronto, London, Sydney, Auckland
www.randomhouse.com

THREE RIVERS PRESS is a registered trademark and the Three Rivers Press colophon is a trademark of Random House, Inc.

Printed in the United States of America

Design by Susan Maksuta

Library of Congress Cataloging-in-Publication Data
Leonhardt, Mary.
    99 ways to get your kids to do their homework : (and not
hate it) / Mary Leonhardt. — 1st ed.
        p. cm.
    1. Homework—Handbooks, manuals, etc.   2. Education—
Parent participation—Handbooks, manuals, etc.   I. Title: Ninety-
nine ways to get your kids to do their homework.   II. Title.
LB1048.L46 2000
372.13'028'1—dc21
                                                    00-028660

ISBN 0-609-80638-6

10 9 8 7 6 5 4 3 2 1
First Edition

Dedicated to my children—
Julie, Tim, and Molly—
for making me realistic about homework.

Special thanks to my students,
for all of their insight and help.

CONTENTS

Introduction   3

Chapter 1: TEN TOP TIPS   7

Chapter 2: TIPS FOR PRESCHOOLERS   23
Help Them Become Absorbed in Projects and Fall in
Love with Books

Chapter 3: ELEMENTARY SCHOOL   37
Help Them Become Independent About Reading and
Doing Homework
    General Guidelines   37
    Problems with Assignments   51
    Problems with Your Child's Performance   57

Chapter 4: JUNIOR HIGH   73
Maintain Interest While Dealing with the Social Scene
    General Guidelines   73
    Making It More Likely Young Teenagers Do Homework   79
    Problems with Classes and Assignments   89
    Problems with Your Child's Ability to Do the Work   93

Chapter 5: HIGH SCHOOL   105
    General Guidelines   105
    Choosing Classes   113
    Roadblocks to High-School Success   118
    College in Mind   124

Chapter 6: A FEW WORDS ABOUT GIFTED CHILDREN   127

99 WAYS

TO GET YOUR KIDS
TO DO THEIR
HOMEWORK

(AND NOT HATE IT)

INTRODUCTION

I've been a teacher for close to thirty years and have written a number of books about how to get kids to love reading and writing. But I think that's too ambitious a goal for homework. *Some* homework children can easily love—assignments that respect their talents, assignments that absorb them and give them the satisfaction of completing an exciting, interesting task—but much homework is pretty dreary. Kids are made to fill out worksheets, write rigid essays, and memorize vocabulary words. Boring. The dog ate it. ZZZzzzzzz.

We all know the conventional advice for getting kids to do this stuff. We should set up a daily schedule for them to follow, make sure they have a quiet area for study, help them keep track of assignments, give them a hand with any difficult work, and check to make sure everything is finished.

And, I guess, with some children this routine works well. I always pictured these happy, compliant children, these competent, successful parents, in my mind when I was trying to get *my* children to do homework. Homework never worked like that in my house.

No, my three children did homework when and where they felt like it—sometimes in front of the television, sometimes in the car on the way to school, sometimes in the kitchen surrounded by comic books and jam sandwiches . . . and sometimes never. I won't soon forget the eighth-grade teacher who informed me that my daughter was getting a D in English because she wasn't answering the comprehension questions, or doing the plot webs, for the stories they were reading in class.

"I know she's reading the stories," the teacher told me, "because she always takes part in the class discussions on them."

"Then, ah . . ." I ventured to ask, "what's the point of the comprehension questions?"

"To make sure they're reading the story," the teacher said promptly, and with no trace of irony.

So I went home and asked Molly why she wasn't doing the questions.

"The stories are interesting, but the questions are dumb," she informed me.

"And the plot web? What's a plot web?" I asked. Somehow, twenty-two years of teaching high-school English had left me without a knowledge of plot webs.

"I don't know. I don't do them," she said definitively.

And she didn't. But you know what? Because she loved reading, and was a very good writer, she did just fine in her high-school English courses. It turned out that she had all the essentials in place for doing well in school, and when the dumb assignments dropped out, as they tend to do the higher up the education ladder kids climb, she didn't have a problem with homework. Not only that, the independent mind that occasionally got her in trouble in elementary and middle school helped her in high school, where she was able to produce some very sophisticated work.

I wasn't surprised, because I understood by then that there was boring, mindless homework—and there was real homework. All of my children tended to do the real homework, and I had decided long ago that that was enough. It enabled me to accept their sometimes less-than-stellar report cards with equanimity. I knew they were acquiring all of the necessary skills that real homework teaches.

And that's what this book is about. The trick to homework, I've figured out, is not to let the bad drive out the good. You can't let the tedium and mindlessness of bad homework assignments contaminate the whole idea of independent work.

While it's very important—crucial for later success in college and in the workplace—for children to acquire the independent habits of work that good school assignments produce, it isn't important that parents hang over children and make sure they do a perfect job on every random worksheet that comes home. In fact, it's counterproductive, because it ensures that kids will begin to hate all homework.

So what *should* parents do? Should they give help? How much? When? These are the issues this book will try to unravel.

In addition, I've included some interviews with high-school students who have had very different experiences with homework over the years. You'll see that almost all kids have ups and downs where homework is concerned, and I think you'll also see that the best thing for a parent to do—in almost all situations—is to give friendly support. Attempts at coercion usually backfire, and end up doing more harm than good.

I'd love to hear from you with more tips or feedback. You can E-mail me at maryl@tiac.net.

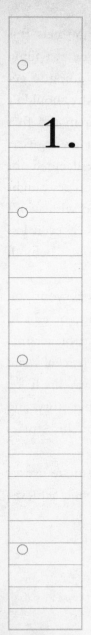

Chapter 1
TEN TOP TIPS

1.

An ability to work independently, to be absorbed and enthusiastic about academic tasks, should be your overriding homework goal for your children.

You need to keep this goal firmly in mind so you won't be tempted to make top grades be your chief goal. Suppose you have a son who is supposed to write a story for his fourth-grade class. He's excited about the assignment and is lying on the floor, pencil in hand, giggling at the silly plot he's making up. That's great. Couldn't be better. Resist the temptation to help him. Of course, the story would be better with your input, but having a terrific story is not your main goal. Having him contentedly working on his own is your goal, and he's doing that.

The problem with helping him is that then the story is not his own, very cool creation. It has your grown-up ideas and constructions. The teacher will probably like it better, but your son won't feel as good about it. And the next time he gets this kind of assignment, he won't be as willing to work on his own. If you're going to get involved and change things, why shouldn't he just give the story to you in the first place? After a while he won't even give a story to you, because he'll have decided not to bother doing it. And then you get caught in the horrible cycle of a child who won't do homework, gets behind, feels even less like doing homework because he's behind, and gets even further behind.

So just admire that silly story your son writes without trying to change or edit it. Let him have his great feeling of accomplishment. He's an author! He can write great, funny stories! That way he'll be enthusiastic about trying another story, and then another, and pretty soon his stories really will be good.

Independence and enthusiasm are everything when it comes to academic achievement.

2.

Make sure your children have the basic abilities in place to be successful in homework.

Essentially this means making sure your children can read and write well. These are the key academic skills that are necessary for success in every subject. You want your children to be avid readers, and to write for fun outside of their school curriculum. See my earlier books *(99 Ways to Get Kids to Love Reading* and *99 Ways to Get Kids to Love Writing)* for suggestions.

Here's the short version: Provide your kids with lots of very high-interest reading they can easily love, such as magazines, comic books, or series books. Don't worry about quality. High-quality books can come later after they've acquired sophisticated reading skills. The same principle holds true for writing. Buy them diaries, show them how to write poems and stories, help them put out a little neighborhood newspaper—things like that. If you can develop a love and habit of reading and writing in your children, skill will follow.

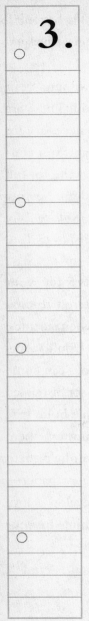

3.

Understand that children are all different and there is no one right way to deal with homework.

Although all children need to become independent about studying, the ways of accomplishing this vary from child to child. My students tell me in great detail how their parents have had to treat their brothers or sisters one way, and them another way. That's okay. Figure out what works best for each one of your children.

Some kids tell me they just want to go up to their room, close the door, and do their homework with no interruptions. Others like to sit at the kitchen table with a friendly parent who is perhaps paying bills or working on a project of her own. Some kids like to do homework right after school. Others have to run around a bit first. Some kids can't motivate themselves until the last minute.

Also—and I know I'm not the first one to notice this—oldest and only children tend to be more conscientious about homework. The danger here is that because pressure and some micromanaging seemed to

work okay with our oldest child, we tend to think it will work with younger siblings— and it almost certainly won't. They tend to be more resistant to parental wishes.

So be flexible. Don't try to fit one child into another child's mold.

4. *But all kids need to know that their parents care about their school performance and are supportive of their academic work.*

This is the theme that comes up again and again when talking with successful students. Their parents didn't check up on them as such, but were full of praise when they succeeded, and sympathetic and helpful when they were having trouble.

Students who didn't feel this support were bitter. One young man wrote: "My parents just try to use fear to motivate me to do homework, yet make no effort to help. . . . They want me to succeed, but only for bragging rights."

The successful students tended to say things like this girl: "If I needed help, then my parents would help me, and they acted interested so that I became interested, too.

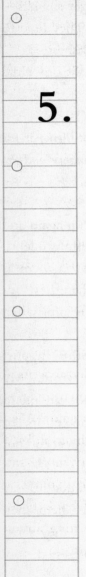

My parents just let me choose whether I wanted to do it, but I did."

So warm, friendly interest: yes. Fear and pressure: no.

5.

Don't worry when they sometimes fail to complete assignments they see as useless.

I had a very interesting discussion with my senior rhetoric class—a class of very advanced students—about homework. Some kids told me they always did every assignment. "I just do it," they'd say. "I don't think about it. I just get it done." Other kids did some picking and choosing, and explained to me that that ability to prioritize was helpful to them in other aspects of their lives. "I pick the assignments that are relevant," one said, "and only do the others if I have to." The young man, already accepted at MIT, explained that, with his outside computer jobs, he didn't have time to do every little task his teachers wanted.

The interesting thing about this discussion was that many of the kids who said they always did every assignment were very cynical about schoolwork. A very bright, successful girl explained to me that she had just completed an American-literature course without reading any of the books. Oh, she read parts of the books, and from the excerpts and class discussions was able to write all of the papers and pass all of the tests. And get an A in the course. But she didn't feel as though she got anything out of it. The kids who were more selective about the assignments they did, on the other hand, often felt that what they were doing was worthwhile.

I'm not sure how this works in other subjects where creativity and original thought might not be as important—such as science and math—but in English I get the best work from students who are not so driven to do every assignment exactly according to specification. The really wonderful writers are usually kids who do their own thing—who change the assignments, or ignore ones they think are dumb, or hand things in late. The best writer I ever had in twenty-eight years didn't do any of the regular assignments I gave. Instead, he handed in notebooks filled with dazzling, breathtaking writing about any subject he felt was important.

The important thing is that your children are absorbed and working on *something*. If the something isn't exactly what the teacher ordered . . . well, maybe she'll realize her assignment wasn't very good to begin with. But your goal is met as long as your children are working.

If your children aren't working at all, of course, then you have a problem.

6. *Do worry if your children are not completing assignments because the assignments are too hard.*

This is the biggest red flag, the most important problem to worry about. Because if homework is too hard, then the work in school is probably too hard also. A child who constantly has to struggle with too-hard work will soon grow to hate school.

I'd do a couple of things here. First of all, ask other parents how their children are doing. Perhaps the problem isn't with your child; possibly the curriculum or teacher is the problem. If a large number of children are having trouble, perhaps you should form a group, and go and visit the teacher or principal.

But suppose most other children are doing fine. Then you need to take some action. I give specific suggestions later, but for now, understand that making a child do homework that is so difficult that he needs extensive help is counterproductive. He won't become independent about studying. He won't become excited and enthusiastic. Before long he'll hate homework, and hate school, too. No one can deal gracefully with spending hours and hours bent over impossible tasks. Only discouragement and anger result.

7. *Don't let their schedules get too crowded.*

I had a mother call me one time to express concern that her son wasn't getting an A in English. "He is really motivated to get all A's this semester," she told me.

"Well," I explained, "he needs to do a good deal of independent reading for me to get an A."

"Oh, he's a ranked tennis player and is on the courts for six hours a day. He doesn't have time to do all that reading," she explained, adding, "but he really needs that A."

Other students tell me that they can't put time into my homework because they have a job, or too active a social life, or are taking too many other courses. And, when I hear about their typical days, I understand their problem. But it's not okay. They are trying to do too many things.

When my older daughter, Julie, who played a varsity sport every season, was in high school, we wouldn't approve any schedule that didn't have at least one study period a day. Nor would we let her work during the school year. We gave her spending money. We were willing to drive old cars and shop in thrift shops so she could devote all of her time to schoolwork, her beloved sports, and some relaxation activities.

Yes, you have to keep relaxation in mind, too. Up through high school even very serious students are really still kids and need a bit of unstructured, goof-off time. Scheduling every minute of their day just leads to stressed-out, or turned-off, kids.

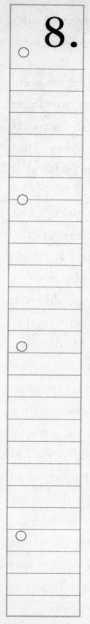

8.

Keep an eye on the relationship your kids have with their teachers.

Children are more likely to work for teachers they like. A warm, nurturing teacher can often pull homework out of the most reluctant kid, while a cold, emotionally battering teacher can discourage and alienate even conscientious students.

Most parents believe they have only minimal control over the teachers their children have, but the reality is that administrators—if pushed hard enough—can be responsive to parental concerns regarding individual teachers. I wouldn't raise the roof over a teacher who was kind and trying, but a little incompetent, but I would go to war over the kind of harsh, dictatorial teachers who discourage kids. They do much harm, both in the school community as a whole and with individual students. If your children run up against this kind of teacher, organize the other parents and demand a change.

9.

Don't overlook medical or emotional problems as a reason for uncompleted homework.

Suppose your daughter is refusing to complete any of her assignments, yet you know she could easily do them. And she seems to like her teachers pretty well. She has plenty of time. But she just isn't succeeding in school.

I'd have a good medical workup first. Maybe she's getting stomachaches every day, or headaches. Perhaps her vision is rapidly changing. Never overlook the obvious.

If she checks out there, you should try to have a therapist evaluate her. Perhaps she's depressed or school-phobic. Maybe she's being harassed by classmates. Sometimes kids have great difficulty confiding problems like this to parents, yet will discuss them with a professional—who, after all, is trained to elicit just these kinds of confidences. And once these problems are understood, much can be done. There are often good community and school support services she can use. Sometimes medication helps. Or sometimes just having problems out in the open is such a relief to kids that they can begin functioning again without a lot of extra help.

The best, most caring parents sometimes have children who are especially vulnerable to life's ups and downs. There is no shame in taking your children for help. There *is* shame in closing your eyes to their need.

10.

Don't punish for uncompleted homework.

In all of my years of teaching, I've never seen punishment be effective in really turning children around and making them act responsibly about their homework. Grounding kids, or restricting their phone time, often results in a short-term gain but a long-term loss. Kids do better for a while, but then are so angry and humiliated that they soon revert to their old, irresponsible ways.

There are enough natural consequences for uncompleted homework, such as a lower grade, embarrassment in class, or the anger of their teacher, that you don't need to add more punishment on top of it. Instead, say something like, "I'm really worried about you. What can I do to help you get your work done?"

And look hard for the reason for the uncompleted work.

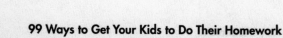

The Kid We All Thought We'd Have

This student loves learning and always did her homework without any prompting at all. In fact, she told me she used to beg her mother sometimes to read her papers. As I'm writing this, she's just been accepted for early admission to Harvard University.

In elementary school I remember having fun. I loved the assignments and projects. Carlisle School was a very homelike environment. I enjoyed going to school every day. I remember always having good teachers. In elementary school I just loved learning. I loved going to school and playing the games. And when you're young you don't see the faults of your teachers. No one struck me as bad. No one let me down. I don't remember bringing work home. In fifth grade I used to do homework while watching TV because I got so bored. Sometimes my mother would read a paper I'd written or look at some illustrations I'd done, but there was never this "Sit down at the table and do your homework." I was the kind of kid who came home and the first thing I'd do was homework. If I did get a lot in elementary school, it didn't strike me as difficult.

Middle school was pretty much the same thing. I never felt overwhelmed except when I had a concert and a softball game. It was very doable. The work wasn't at all challenging. I'm very competitive, always have been. When you're getting hundreds on all the tests, there's no further you can go. The key is having the challenge that is just right. That's something Carlisle did well. My mom has always said I've been a competitive person. I just end up doing it. I've done some illustrated posters for my projects here and I just get carried away. In music I like competition, too. I don't know if the music or competition came first. I was also very into sports up until the ninth grade, basketball and softball.

Freshman year was a cinch. Sophomore year was stressful, but junior year was very easy until the second half of the year when it got nuts. But in high school my parents never pushed me. In fact, most of the time they're saying, "Why are you still doing work this late?" I have my mom read my papers and she mostly says they're fine. I just have her read them to build confidence. If someone tells me they don't like something, I get very defensive. I don't see my family very often. When I'm not at school, which is rare, I'm in my room till all hours of the night. My mom always tells me that my brother was the type of person that if he had a three-page paper due, he'd increase the font, triple-space it. "So," she says, "how did we end up with you?"

In high school the love of learning has dwindled a little. I feel like my work has gone downhill. But I always feel like that. Nothing I do is ever good enough. I'm a perfectionist in a bad way.

When I do a group project, I do much more and I feel terrible because the rest of my group just gets pulled through the whole thing. High-school culture doesn't support creativity. High school in general doesn't understand that there are some teachers who will just expect to get a mediocre paper and will get frustrated with a longer paper. With my style I get people who love it or hate it.

Chapter 2
TIPS FOR PRESCHOOLERS
Help Them Become Absorbed in Projects and Fall in Love with Books

11.

Provide an enriched home environment.

If you want to guess how a group of children will do in school, the most reliable way isn't to look at the school they are attending, or the teachers, or the curriculum, but at their homes. Socioeconomic status is the best predictor of future school success. Children who do well academically tend to come from homes with educated parents who are making a good income.

But I think any parents can replicate this kind of environment. You need a house filled with books—and library books work as well as expensive, new ones. You need to talk with your children and listen to them. Take them places. Museums are great, but children often learn as much from simply being allowed to be part of your daily activities. Take them into work sometimes, if you can. Take them to ball games and plays; local ones are fine and inexpensive. Take them to playgrounds and swimming pools. Try to involve them in any activity you enjoy, be it fishing or planting a garden.

All of these experiences enlarge their minds, and give them a wider framework of knowledge. Later, when they study biology at school, for example, they'll remember fishing with you, and the whole subject will be much more interesting for them. We're most interested in things we already know a little about.

12.

Make sure your home is a relaxed, loving, child-centered place.

I know not everyone agrees with me on this, but almost thirty years of teaching, and paying attention to the home lives of my students, has convinced me: Kids who are trusted and treated kindly do better than kids subjected to strict rules and discipline.

Sometimes my classes get into debates over the best way to raise children, and it invariably happens that a student will start saying that *he* was always being grounded, and maybe even spanked, and he believed that was the best way to raise children. The kid who argues this is *never* an excellent student—and is often a really terrible student. I remember once a young man (a poor student) was arguing that his parents beat him when he cut class and saying that was a good thing, when another young man (an excellent student) put up his hand and said, "But my parents have never beaten me, and I've never cut class." Exactly.

So start early treating your children with respect and gentleness. It will pay off big-time when they're in school, never mind throughout their lives.

13. *Pay special attention to helping preschoolers develop a love of reading and writing.*

Again, I talk much more about this in my other books, but basically, you want to surround your young children with all kinds of books, and you want to encourage any writing or drawing they are willing to do. Read to them every day, and then encourage them to tell *you* stories. Take them to the library. Buy them books of their own—at supermarkets, garage sales, flea markets—any-where. Children's magazines, comic books, Disney books—any kind of reading material they can easily love is great to have around.

Children who begin school able to follow a story read to them, and interested in look-ing at books themselves, are way ahead of kids who aren't. If you can do a little early reading instruction, that's fine, too. Just keep it light and fun. The minute your child balks, back off.

14.

While your children are young, teach them to treat any adult who is hardworking with great respect. This will help them acquire a work ethic.

This is really important in your family. If you're fortunate enough to be able to hire household help, be sure your children treat these workers with the greatest respect. Be sure that they appreciate the work that each parent does. All of the working adults your kids come in contact with—cashiers, policemen, doctors—should be admired for the hard work and effort they put into their jobs.

I think most of us do this automatically, but it's easy to forget, when we're tired and rushed, to accord that extra level of politeness to people waiting on us or working for us. But since we want our children to understand that *effort* is praiseworthy in itself, we need to remember. It's why kids coming from abusive homes have an extra hurdle to jump before they can start doing well. Since an abuser is rarely the one doing all the work, children from these homes are used to seeing the hard work of victims pay off in threats and more abuse—a terrible lesson to learn.

15.

Don't organize or direct their play at home; instead, just give suggestions.

You want your children to be able to work independently at school, so it's important they learn to play independently at home. When they're in a class of twenty-five children, they won't have an adult directing their every move.

So have toys and dress-up clothes and crayons and dolls around at home, but don't spend too much time down on the floor with them. Be working on a project yourself in their general vicinity, and make occasional suggestions like, "Oh, I wonder if this box would make a good dollhouse. And I have some old wrapping paper that would make great wallpaper." If the suggestion is greeted with enthusiasm, fine, but don't get involved with much of the actual construction yourself.

(Of course, my kids would have said something like, "Nah. Dollhouses are dumb. But let's take it outside, fill it with dirt, get all Mother's silver spoons from the dining room . . .")

16. *Make sure they get used to playing with other children.*

I think the popular image of the smart nerd who doesn't get along with his classmates is largely a myth. Generally, socially adept children also do better academically. I think they're happier and more comfortable, for one thing. For another, much schoolwork these days involves working with classmates in groups.

So somehow you have to arrange for your

children to spend lots of time with other kids. If they're in day care or nursery school, then they're with other children all day. If not, you'll need to meet other mothers and set up play dates and park excursions. Try to expose them to a variety of children so they become comfortable with other cultures and other family interactions.

17.

You may need to teach them strategies for dealing with bullies, or for not being bullies themselves.

While I think it's generally better to let children work out their differences among themselves, sometimes kids need help, especially if they are falling into the pattern of often being a bully or victim.

For children who are being victimized, try to simplify the play situation. Suppose your son is being picked on. Try to arrange things so he is playing with only one or two gentle friends at a time. As he gains confidence, gradually enlarge the group. And try teaching him ways of standing up for himself, as bullies don't enjoy having a victim suddenly turn on them.

If you have a daughter who screams at and hits other children, you need to work with her on finding other outlets for her anger and need to control a situation. A token system that rewards her for putting her anger into words, instead of into action, for example, might help.

If these interaction problems persist, I'd get professional help. Behavior problems inevitably spill over and cause problems in school. And, of course, there are also all kinds of other reasons for getting your child this help.

18.

Make sure your children get used to having adults other than you sometimes care for them.

It's important for kids to get used to adults who do things a little differently from their parents. This gives them the flexibility to deal with the variety of teachers they'll have. I don't think it's bad at all for kids to see that some adults will insist they wear jackets outside when it's cold, and others won't. Some adults insist children be very respectful, saying "sir" and "ma'am," while others prefer a more casual form of address. A child who feels comfortable with these different expectations will have a much easier time in a classroom.

The other reason for exposing children to a variety of adults is that children need to learn to get along with adults who don't have the emotional attachment to them that their parents do.

19.

Keep in mind that making children lovable is as important as making them feel loved.

It's easy, as parents, to overlook this. *We* love our children and assume that everyone will love them. But look around at the children of your friends. Are they all as lovable as your kids? No? Then maybe other parents don't find your children lovable, either.

Lovable is important, because it means your kids realize they are not the center of the universe. They realize that other people have needs and concerns. They realize they have to put themselves out for others.

The homework reason for ensuring this is that lovable kids get more teacher help, get more help from their friends, and feel better about themselves, in the bargain. Their social self-confidence spills over in a general energy and enthusiasm for life (and school-work).

20. Discourage reliance on television, videos, or computers for entertainment.

Many of my best high-school students had their television time severely restricted when they were young. I don't think there's any way around the fact that this lack of television and videos was a big factor in their passion for reading, and their knowledge and interest in a wide variety of subjects.

That isn't to say I don't have other excellent students who had television available but developed good academic interests and abilities anyway. So there's no one right answer. But if your children are not interested in books, don't know how to amuse themselves, and are spending hours and hours a week in front of the tube, I'd start turning it off. The thing to be careful of in a house without any television is making your children feel isolated and different. I don't think that's good, either.

As for computers, I wouldn't jump on this bandwagon yet. I think little kids need to be outside playing, or inside listening to stories or building forts under the dining-room table. Watching preschoolers bent over a keyboard chills me.

A Horrible Childhood Experience

I had this student in my American-literature class. I asked the kids about homework one day, and she started laughing and said, "You have to talk with me." Since she was an excellent student (and diver, who had won first place in the state the previous two years), I was curious. At this writing, she's just been accepted early to Brown University.

In elementary school homework was awful. My mom and dad would sit me down at the dining-room table by myself. They'd put a timer next to me and say, "You have to have all your homework done by seven o'clock"—or they'd take away a privilege and yell at me. We'd spend weekends at this table and my dad would sit over me and say, "This is how you do it. What's the answer?" All through elementary school I wouldn't do my homework. I hated it. Once I got a D in math and my parents freaked out.

Then I moved up here for middle school and they didn't give grades and they didn't give that much homework. I plain old didn't care. I did my work, but I didn't care and I didn't put any effort into it.

Ninth grade I began to realize that it matters and it helps, but I still slacked off all the time. In tenth grade I had at least four parent conferences a semester. I'd go into my math class and say, "I hate math and I'm going to fail the test." Then I tried harder. I didn't study a lot, but I did do my homework. I realized homework relates to diving, that if you work at it and pay attention, you'll learn things. In tenth grade I won states [placed first in the state diving competition].

In junior year I picked up my act a lot. I figured out that TV doesn't matter. I figured out I just have to do it. Most kids say they have to stay up all night. Baloney. I get home at eight o'clock from diving and I'm in bed by ten-thirty—sometimes eleven or eleven-thirty. It's all about managing your time. Days that I don't have diving, I go to bed late. I take a bubble bath, watch TV, and do anything I can to avoid homework. I figure I have all night and go to bed really late. Free time is a killer.

I think parents forcing their kids to do it doesn't work. I just resisted harder. The more they sat with me, the more I resisted. It made me feel like I was no good. As long as kids are trying, it should be okay. When I didn't do well, I'd think, Oh my God, I'm letting everybody down. I think little kids do need to be taught, but my parents went too far with it. After a while, I said, "You need to leave me alone." Kids need to figure it out by themselves.

21.

Avoid giving your children the idea that there is only one right way to do things.

I know, with small children, it's tempting to say things like, "This is the way to arrange things in the refrigerator" or "Towels need to be folded this way." But I think it's much better, in areas where choice is perfectly fine, to say, "Some people like to put the milk on the top shelf, and some people like to put it on the door. Let's see. Where should we put it?"

That way children become more confident about figuring out things themselves, a crucial ability in doing any serious academic work. I've seen kids almost paralyzed by worry that they aren't doing an assignment "right." Even if your children get an occasional fanatic teacher, over their entire academic and professional careers, they will do much better if they look at a task and say, "Well, I guess I could do it like this, or like this . . . or even like *this*." They'll feel more confident about starting an assignment, and end up doing a more interesting, creative job.

Chapter 3
ELEMENTARY SCHOOL:
Help Them Become Independent About Reading and Doing Homework

GENERAL GUIDELINES

22.

You may have to help your children get organized when they first have homework assignments.

If you have children who come right home, excited about having homework and ready to start, then just play the part of an admiring audience. "Oh yes, you're so big now. And I know you'll do a great job with it because you're so smart."

But if your daughter's homework is out-of-sight and so out-of-mind in her book bag and she's heading out the door to climb trees, you might gently ask, "And so when do you think will be the best time for you to do your homework? I know that you're so good in school that you'll want to do really well with your homework, too. You could do it now or after dinner."

Gently is the key word here. You want your children to be independent about homework as soon as possible, so make sure that they understand it's their responsibility (not yours!) right from the beginning.

23.

As long as they are happily working, leave them alone.

They're learning independence and building their ability to concentrate. So even if they are doing the assignment all wrong—and therefore not learning much spelling at the moment, for example—I'd lay low. Presumably, their teacher will notice.

The reason for leaving them alone is that an independent spirit, a willingness to figure out things, and the ability to focus are the gold coins that eventually make kids excellent students.

24.

If your children ask for help, try to make it seem as though they're teaching you, rather than the other way around.

For example, suppose your son wants help with his math homework. Rather than sitting down and immediately pointing out to him the correct way to solve the problem, I'd say something like, "Oh gee, it's been a long time since I've done this kind of math. How did your teacher say to set up the problem?" Then try to gently lead your son into figuring out himself the way to proceed.

Sometimes, of course, this doesn't work and your son will need more direct help. A little bit of explicit help is fine, but if it becomes a nightly thing, either your son has stopped trying himself or the work is too hard. If he simply can't do the work himself, look at the sections on problems for tips on how to proceed. If he's just stopped trying, you need to turn back the homework responsibility to him.

25.

Gradually wean too-dependent children from your help.

For example, help your son with the first math problem, get him started on the second, and then remember something you absolutely have to do at the moment. "Oh, just keep going," tell him, "and I'll be back in a minute." When you come back, lavishly praise any work that he's done himself. Help him finish his work then, and the next night find another excuse to stay away even longer. The goal, of course, is eventually to have him doing all of the work himself.

I wouldn't be above a little duplicity, either. Once he's gained some confidence and is really trying, make an obvious mistake when helping him. If he catches it, look chagrined and say, "You know, I think you're getting better at this stuff than I am."

You'll be amazed at how quickly kids start believing they are much more competent than you. And that's okay. They'll grow up and understand more someday. But for now, believing that *they* are best at doing their work is a powerful motivator.

26.

The ultimate goal is to have your children do work completely on their own, without any structure or help from you.

Notice that the goal isn't to have them do a perfect job on homework. Having home-work done right isn't nearly as important as having it done independently. Keep saying to yourself, It's *grade school.* Who cares if he gets an A on homework? It's much more important that children learn to handle assignments on their own.

I really think conventional wisdom—that has parents setting the time for doing homework, checking homework, signing off on homework—is wrong. It transfers final responsibility for homework completely to the parents, when it's the children who need to accept that responsibility.

If you allow this to happen, after a while, kids won't do any homework without all kinds of parental and school pressure. Don't get started down this road. Right from the beginning, make it clear to your children that *their* homework isn't something you're going to worry about. Why should you? They're bright, responsible kids, right? And even if you secretly think they're not very responsible, treating them as if they are will help make them so.

27.

Do provide your children with any books or materials they need for homework.

In my house, this usually meant that about eight o'clock on a snowy, cold January night, one of my daughters would remember that she needed poster board and markers for a project due the next morning. Or my son would need poker chips for math. Or someone would need a particular book. They always remembered at the last minute and they always needed it *right then*.

While conventional wisdom would dictate you say, "Tough luck, you should have thought of it sooner," I always tried to oblige, if I could. I rationalized that there was no question of my actually *doing* the homework. It was still their province. But by grabbing my car keys for the ice-cold trip, I was showing them how important I thought homework was. And how important they were.

28. *Keep casual track of how your children are doing.*

I stress "casual" here. Have a general idea of what they're studying. Pay a bit of attention to their relationship with their teacher. Make lots of positive comments about how smart they are, and how proud of them you are.

But don't be calling up the school all the time to check up on them. Don't insist on checking, or even seeing, their completed homework. Don't let them think that their worth to you depends on the kind of grades they get. You love them, and you're interested in their schoolwork like you're interested in everything else they do—but you respect them as competent, conscientious people and don't need to oversee everything they do.

29. Never let any of their assignments interfere with their independent reading.

I can't stress this enough. If kids in elementary school are spending hours on endless school assignments, and not feeling that they have any time to read for pleasure, what's going to happen to them in junior high and high school? Reading assignments will be even longer then, and they will be less and less able to do them.

Elementary school is the key time for children to develop a love and habit of reading. Don't let anything interfere with that. No homework assignment can begin to

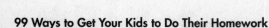

compete with a fascinating book when it comes to developing sophisticated reading skills.

30. *Encourage independent writing as well.*

The biggest reason for doing poorly in an English class and, by college, in many other classes as well, is an inability to write well. You can head this off by encouraging your children to write for pleasure at home. I go into great detail on how to accomplish this in my book *99 Ways to Get Kids to Love Writing,* but here's the short version:

Keep in mind that any kind of writing is good, and creative writing is especially good, as it develops fluency and a writer's voice. So be very encouraging about any attempts. Help your kids make little books, put out newspapers, write poems for their grandparents. Look for writing groups at your local libraries. Check out magazines, like *Stone Soup,* that carry children's writing. If you can give your kids the idea that writing is fun, they'll be way ahead of their classmates.

And If You're Lucky Enough to Have an Artist

I had this student, a wonderful writer, in my senior rhetoric class last spring. Notice how his parents nurtured his art talent and allowed him to work out homework issues himself. He's at the Rhode Island School of Design this year—one of the top art schools in the country.

I was the kid who was, "Oh wow, we get to do homework now." I was really smart in elementary school. I'm just finding that out because we got back all our old records when we graduated. They said I was more intelligent than most adults. I needed to be challenged. I started reading a lot in third grade. My mom's a huge reader and we'd go to the library and pick out books.

I took a lot of art classes at the Emerson Umbrella, and just about every summer until my sophomore summer I was off doing art things. Horizons up in the mountains, techie art—glass-blowing, metal, fabrics—I loved that stuff. It was an intensive training program. You had long studio and open studio. Sort of an artist commune. I did that two years in a row, eighth-grade summer and freshman summer. MSSA [Middlesex Summer Arts Camp]—I was doing that when I was nine or ten. I did that two or three years.

My mother early in sixth grade checked homework and then she assumed I was all right and stayed off my back. In eighth grade I was actually doing all my homework, but some was getting done early in the morning. And I was doing a lot of art on my own—I had my own acrylic painting studio in the basement. I set that up my seventh-grade year. I cleared out a nice area by the window and set out my easels and table. My parents were very supportive. In middle school art helped me relax and get my mind cleared for doing other schoolwork. I was also reading a lot then. A lot of Stephen King. Vonnegut. Clive Barker. Asimov.

I loved art in high school—the concept of study or free blocks and you could go in the art rooms and do more work. And I got to do the computer art, which was great. Junior year I probably had more problems keeping up with stuff. Every quarter I'd pick something up and something else would fall—like the Charlie Chaplin thing with the suitcases. He picks up one and drops the other. I'd get a low grade in math, so I'd say, "Buckle down and get this done." Then the next quarter something else would be a problem. My parents got kind of upset, and I'd try to organize myself. A few times early on at the end of sophomore year they tried grounding me. But they were really involved with my brothers, who didn't get good grades. I guess they finally figured they'd leave this one alone.

You have to think the work you're doing is important. I'm going to RISD and thinking of doing illustration, or something more conducive to theater. I'm doing lots of stuff with puppetry. I also work now designing and teaching Web design.

31.

See if you can keep your children going to the library.

Most kids love the library as preschoolers, when they go to story hour, and check out piles of picture books. But when the family gets so busy with a regular school day, it's easy to let the library habit slip. I'd work hard to prevent that from happening.

Realistically, you probably can't afford to buy all of the books that you need to develop an avid reader. In elementary school, avid readers can go through almost a book a day. And that's *good*. You want that to happen. You also want children to stay comfortable and familiar with libraries. Then when they start getting research assignments, they will have some idea how to proceed.

So make a library visit be a regular part of your schedule. And encourage your children to ask the librarians for suggestions when they can't find a book they like. Not only will they get good advice, they will learn how friendly and helpful most librarians are. Personally, I think librarians are a huge, underrated resource, and for the kids in this country who are avid readers, credit should go more to librarians (and parents) than to educators or politicians.

32.

Spend as much money on books and other enrichment materials (like chemistry sets, etc.) as you spend on sports.

While sports are wonderful in all kinds of ways for children—physically, emotionally, and socially—you are teaching skewed values if you're willing to spend hundreds, or thousands, of dollars a year on uniforms and league fees and summer camps, but not on subscriptions to magazines your children like, or the latest book in a series they're reading, or visits to museums or historical sites.

We understand that interest and commitment from parents help kids achieve in sports. The same holds true for academic areas. And I would argue that a love of reading and a passionate interest in history or math or science will help your kids more in the long run than an expertise in soccer.

Of course, the ideal is that sports and schoolwork never become an either/or situation. The self-discipline and joy that kids get from sports should spill over and make them better students, and a lively, creative intelligence will make them better athletes.

33.

Keep firmly in mind that grades don't count in elementary school; skill level counts.

What matters is your children's ability to do the work. If your daughter is reading on a tenth-grade level and can effortlessly do the assigned math, I seriously doubt that any school will try to make her repeat fourth grade—even if she never did one homework assignment. On the other hand, if she sweated every night over every stupid worksheet sent home, and still reads only on a second-grade level, she probably will be held back.

And even if grades *do* count—if, for example, you're trying to get your child accepted into a selective high school—they don't count as much as basic reading and writing ability. Few schools will turn down students who score sky-high on standardized tests, no matter what their grades are.

So focus on getting your kids to become avid readers. Help get them really interested in science and history. Let them see how math is important in everyday life. And—if there's time left—encourage them to do their homework.

34.

Pressure for high grades can lead to all kinds of problems, even in elementary school.

Students are telling me that cheating is starting really early now. Kids in fourth or fifth grade are copying one another's homework or cheating on tests. I find that students who regularly cheat become completely cynical about learning and, as the years go on, become almost impossible to teach. All of their energy goes into planning how to get around an assignment. Plus a teacher never has any real idea of what the student knows or doesn't know. And these practical problems with cheating don't even take into account the moral issues.

So praise your children for the right reasons: for working hard, for developing an interest in some area—and always, always for reading.

PROBLEMS WITH ASSIGNMENTS

35.

If your kids are getting too much homework too soon, protest.

I can hardly believe some of the stories parents tell me—although I'm sure they're true. I hear about second and third graders getting hours and hours of homework every night. What can these teachers be thinking of?

If this is happening, you have to take some action. Otherwise, either your kids get in the habit of never completing homework (good to avoid, if you can) or the time they might have spent with the family, or involved with other meaningful pursuits, is lost to the stress of homework. The problem is even worse for the children with after-school programs, who can't even start their homework until the evening, when everyone is tired and grouchy. And as for extra, independent reading—forget it.

A group is always more effective protesting than a single parent, so try to organize other parents. Then talk with the teacher first. If that doesn't work, go to the principal. If that doesn't work, I'd keep going up the ladder to the assistant superintendent, the superintendent, and then the school committee. As a last resort, your group can start writing letters to the local paper.

Of course, the homework load has to be really unreasonable to go to these lengths. But if it is, don't hesitate.

36. *If your children are given ridiculously hard assignments, still do as little as possible to help them.*

Unfortunately, with all of the emphasis on standards and testing, some teachers are giving assignments that are simply off the wall. One mother told me that her third-grade son had to read a chapter of *Charlotte's Web* every night and take extensive notes. He couldn't begin to do it himself, so they were both spending hours every night on the book (which they had both, predictably, started to hate).

Now really: assigning third graders to take extensive notes on a novel? That's absurd, as the mother well knew. But she felt in a bind. Her son couldn't do the assignment without her help, and so she felt obliged to work along with him.

However, I would counsel her not to. Let him do his best by himself, and if the teacher calls to complain, explain that the assignment is too hard for him. Suggest that it's probably too hard for most of the class, and anyone turning in a good job is probably getting extensive parental help. Also, tell her the assignment is boring and tedious and will turn kids off to reading.

But, at all costs, don't do the work for him. There is no future in that for your child, and if the teacher sees completed work coming in, she'll keep assigning it.

37.

Don't feel that you have to do every parent-participation assignment.

On the whole, if you and your children are enthusiastic, it's fine to do cooperative assignments. But I'm hearing stories about kids being sent home almost every night with directions for extensive parent-help projects. One single mother was telling me how she dreaded school starting in September because of this. She worked hard all day and then had to spend most of her evening doing these school assignments with her daughter.

What I dislike about a heavy dose of this kind of assignment is the assumption that unless schools mandate it, parents will not be educationally involved with their children. This single mother read to her daughter, joined the science museum so she could take her daughter and friends on school holidays, was active with her in many mother-daughter activities—and the school was making her do worksheets?

So if the assignments are nonintrusive and enjoyable, fine. If not, I wouldn't hesitate to write a nice note to your child's teacher saying that, unfortunately, other duties called. I don't think much good can come out of daily work-together sessions that you dislike and simply don't have time for. Once in a while you can fake it, and act enthusiastic. But practically every day?

38.

Even if your children are supposed to get their completed homework signed by you, don't bug them about doing it.

This is the new thing: In many schools parents have to sign homework, testifying that it's complete. I think that this mandate gives many parents the worry that somehow it's *their* homework—and they'd better make really sure it gets done.

But micromanaging homework always carries a price tag: Kids resent your interference and become even less motivated to do assignments themselves.

No, I'd be very casual and forgetful about this parent-signing thing. Be upstairs folding clothes, or down in the workshop sorting nails. Let them find you, and when they do, ask if they would like you to look the homework over. If they say no, but you have to sign that the work is complete, then say, "Oh, okay. Just assure me that you did everything." Believe what they tell you, and sign.

Because there is no future in any other course of action. If you don't trust them and insist on checking it yourself, they'll become more and more alienated from you. And if that happens, a bit of uncompleted homework will be the least of your problems.

Although the popular perception is that kids are quick to take advantage of trusting, loving parents, I find the exact opposite to be the case.

39.

If your children aren't getting any homework—or only getting very little—be grateful.

A common response, when I ask my best students about elementary-school homework, is that they don't remember having much. Maybe they just didn't do it, or maybe they really were assigned very little. But the result was that they spent hours and hours reading, or writing little stories, or making up science experiments—or doing any number of activities that have resulted in them being excellent high-school students.

You do want to be sure your children can absorb themselves in academic projects, but you don't need formally assigned school homework to do this. In fact, it's probably easier without it.

PROBLEMS WITH YOUR CHILD'S PERFORMANCE

If your child is completing the important, interesting assignments but "forgetting" the tedious, busy-work assignments, look the other way.

40.

I wouldn't actively encourage this kind of behavior, but I wouldn't make a big deal out of it, either, especially if your child is doing a lot of reading and other academic-type things on his own. Don't protect him from the natural consequences of his refusal to do certain assignments. If he gets a lower grade, or has to stay in at recess and do the assignment—well, that's a choice he's made.

But don't you add punishment and pressure on top of the school's.

When High Expectations Work

This student was in my senior rhetoric class when we did this interview, and he is now at the Massachusetts Institute of Technology. His parents are from Taiwan, and I think this interview shows that it wasn't just the parents' high expectations and work ethic that enabled him to do so well, but their flexibility, trust, and help as well.

I remember my dad read to me as a child, in English and Chinese, every night. I shared a room with my sister, and one night I was working my way through this book and he was helping me, and my sister said, "Can you stop? I want to go to sleep." And he said, "No, this is important."

There was always the expectation that the homework needs to be done. But I didn't have that much in elementary school, and most of it was fun stuff, so it was not much of a problem to do. And it helped that I had an older sibling who was very hardworking, so I could see that's what you do.

Reading was the biggest thing I did in middle school. A friend got me into fantasy. It's great because it's really easy to read long strings of books. He got me started on the Xanth series. Fantasy makes you read more. In middle school I read a book a night. But homework was easy. It was so easy in middle school to rattle off straight A's. There wasn't much pressure from school, but there was at home.

That's the difference with Asian families. It's always expected that you're going to be working hard. My parents would tell stories about their childhood. They grew up in poverty and worked so hard to become students in America. When you come from that, it's harder to say, "I didn't work hard." I always looked up to my dad.

It's not like they're always on my back. They never said, "Show me your homework assignment" or even asked about report cards. They'd just believe me when I said I was getting straight A's. There was some positive incentive. You got their approval and that was important.

In high school when the work started getting challenging and difficult and there was more of it, the model broke down. My sister was always a high achiever, and that unstructured model worked for her. It didn't work for me when I had way more work and it was more difficult. Freshman year I started having trouble in geometry, and then sophomore year it broke down completely. I had no idea in math. It took quite a bit sophomore year when it was just totally bad—it took that wake-up call for them and me to realize what I was doing wasn't working. We had heart-to-heart discussions. I needed them to show more outward support for me. They started to actively ask about my homework, and that helped. Before tests I'd bring my homework own and they'd go over chapter by chapter. I'd do it with my mom, who is really good in math. They would sit down and go through and make sure I knew it.

I'd always do homework. I'd never not do homework. My sister would go home after school and do it. I would go home, watch TV or something. Both of my parents worked, so I knew that that time was my time to goof off. When my parents got home, I'd go up and do my homework.

But I think you can't force it on a kid. He has to want to do it.

41.

If your child is completing the class work but not much of the homework, I still wouldn't be too worried.

Suppose your son does very well on the work he's given in class, and spends most of his time home reading and building Lego rocket ships. Fundamentally, I wouldn't worry; he's reading, he's getting absorbed in projects, he's doing the work in school. But he may be seriously annoying his teacher. Of course, the reason he's probably not doing homework is that he's bored by it. The teacher is probably seriously annoying him as well.

I think I'd lay low on this one and try not to get caught in the crossfire. Your son needs to learn at some point that other people will set agendas that he doesn't like but for all kinds of reasons will have to follow. Maybe this is the time. Maybe not. But again, I can assure you that my high-school classroom is filled with excellent students who somehow managed to do little or no homework in elementary school.

42.

Children who are having trouble with the schoolwork as well as the homework should be assessed.

Because of Public Law 94-142 schools are required to evaluate any child who is failing and then, if necessary, offer special ed services. Don't be afraid of taking advantage of this law.

For example, suppose your daughter seems to be reading okay but won't do any of the worksheets for reading or for math. Her teacher says that she's just lazy, since she clearly can read the material. Maybe she *can* clearly do the assignment, but you still want an assessment. Perhaps she's a perfectionist and afraid to put that first word on the paper. Maybe she has physical problems with handwriting. Maybe she can *read* the story but doesn't understand it well enough to answer the questions.

You can't solve a problem, after all, until you know exactly what it is.

43.

Understand that emotional problems are every bit as debilitating and difficult to overcome as academic ones.

Suppose the testing done at school suggests that your daughter is very anxious. It's tempting to tell her just to relax and stop worrying about school, but often advice isn't enough. She may need a therapist to help her overcome her anxiety. Or you may benefit from some counseling on ways to help her. Some children seem to get thrown more easily by life's ups and downs, and may require special help to keep going.

Check out the kinds of services your school offers, and if they aren't enough, ask a counselor or teacher you trust for a recommendation of another place to go for help.

44.

A learning disability is also a very real problem that needs to be addressed.

Suppose it turns out that your daughter has a very poor auditory memory. I find that students with this difficulty often have trouble with reading comprehension, particularly when the class starts reading books with no pictures. Students with poor visual memories usually have trouble with note-taking. Their handwriting is often poor, and writing demands so much concentration that they stop listening—and listening is the real way they learn. Students with attention deficit disorder (ADD) get distracted by little things other kids don't even notice.

There are many good ways to test and document these disabilities, and I find that it's often a relief to a student to finally know what's been causing the problem.

45.

Schools are required to make accommodations for students with disabilities.

Under both the special education law (PL 94-142) and the Americans With Disabilities Act, schools are required to make accommodations for disabled students. Both physical and mental disabilities come under these laws.

This means you have real clout when dealing with your children's school. Don't be afraid to ask for a meeting with your child's teachers, guidance counselor, and any other appropriate staff members. At the first meeting you should discuss a specific plan to deal with the problem.

46.

The general principle for remediation is: You want a solution that keeps the student as independent as possible, while teaching the student strategies for coping with the disability.

Under the special education law, schools are required to make up an Individual Education Plan (IEP) for all disabled students. The plan lists the accommodations and special help your child will receive.

For example, suppose it turns out that your daughter has a poor auditory memory, and so has trouble remembering a story well enough to answer questions on it. A good accommodation for a younger child would be to give her books with pictures, or comic books, for a while so she has the pictures to help her. Then gradually she can be weaned off these and get used to books with fewer and fewer pictures, until the point when she can understand and remember stories without any visual help. With an older child you can look for books that are of extremely high interest for her so she can better follow and remember them.

This kind of solution ensures that your daughter is reading independently, is having success, and is developing better reading comprehension.

With a very anxious child you might suggest that work be broken up into very small pieces so she can do just a little and then get positive feedback—which will encourage her to do more. Little things like giving her permission to work with a friend might help. Or you might need major changes, such as a transfer to a more easygoing teacher. But while she's working out her anxiety issues with a therapist, the school should make whatever accommodations it can to help her function better right away.

47.

Don't be intimidated by the educational specialists.

Generally I find special education teachers and guidance counselors to be down-to-earth and genuinely helpful. But you may have the misfortune to come across some who are not. Don't be afraid to bring your own common sense to bear on the issues.

For example, if your daughter can't keep up with the required reading, a specialist may suggest that she listen to the book on tape. But your common sense tells you that if she just listens to books on tape, her reading will never get any better. She needs to *read*. So insist that she be given—or better yet, helped to find—books that are really interesting to her and that are written on her reading level.

48. *Homework compliance should improve when school becomes more comfortable.*

I really think most kids want to do well, and when they *can* do the homework, they will—as long as everyone is encouraging and supportive. But again, your real issue should be that your children are doing the work in school, and reading and being involved in academic-type projects at home. If they are also doing all of their homework in addition to this, well . . . you were born under a lucky star, that's all.

49.

As a last resort, try a reward system.

While I don't like reward systems as a general rule, since they involve a parent much too closely in something that should be a child's responsibility, sometimes a situation is bad enough that a reward system is the lesser evil. So if you have a child—let's say your son—who is doing very little work at home or at school, and if you can't find any apparent reason for this lack of effort, then try rewards.

Keep these general guidelines in mind: Present the reward system as something that will help him. Say something like, "I know you're having trouble remembering to do this schoolwork. Let's figure out a way to help you get settled and start working." Then work with him in devising the system. For example, should you use tokens to show how much time was spent working? What kind of rewards will work best as motivators? And finally—and most important—reward effort, not achievement. Thus, you might give him a token (and a smile and a hug) for every fifteen minutes spent bent over books, but not for the grade that homework assignment gets. You want your child to feel in control of doing well, and effort is something he has control over. Plus, a habit of working is more valuable in the long run than any specific grades earned.

50.

If, after your best efforts, you have a child who is still not doing the work at school or at home, consider drastic solutions.

You don't want to let a situation like this go on too long, as it is very demoralizing for a child. *Something* is very wrong. Redouble your efforts to find out what the source of the trouble is. A medical problem? An emotional problem? A learning disability? A really poor school situation?

If the problem is the school, you should consider moving your child. I know this isn't an easy solution, but a really horrific school year can cause lasting damage. If the problem turns out to be a disability of some kind, go all out to find the best help you can. Don't let people tell you that you just have a lazy child. In close to thirty years of teaching, I have yet to meet a child who, deep down inside, didn't want to succeed and be one of the "smart" kids.

Emotional Issues Can Overwhelm an Ability to Do Homework

This student is one of the best writers I've ever had. Even though she is having trouble with her other homework at the moment, she is so bright and literate that I'm sure she'll end up doing very well. I think she is right for putting most of her energy into recovering from a very debilitating eating disorder.

In elementary school I always did homework. I didn't want to do it to learn, but I was really scared of disappointing my teachers. A number of my teachers were very concerned about me because I was very different from other children. I remember my fifth-grade teacher told my mother I wouldn't succeed in life and my mom and dad were bad parents because they let us think what we wanted to think and do what we wanted to do. She was always upset I was never doing the class work because it was so easy for me. I would make up my own problems, but the teacher didn't like that I wasn't following the curriculum.

In sixth grade I started being very popular, and then one day my friends decided they didn't like me and I had no friends. I really suffered from it. I figured it was all my fault and I was a bad person and I lost my sense of self. My grades were really bad in sixth grade. In seventh grade I decided that since I didn't have the same friends and I was worth less, at least I could do well in school, so I got straight A's. In eighth grade the friends that ditched me realized I was smart and interesting and came back. I hated middle school, absolutely hated it. Although I was very insecure, my parents thought I was fine since my grades were so good.

Freshman year my parents got divorced and it was a bad year. My grades slowly declined as I turned more and more of my attention to my eating disorder. Right now I do the big projects of homework, but the little assignments I never complete. I listen to my Spanish teacher tell me every week that my homework grade of zero is really bringing down my grades, but I still don't care. I work hard in the subjects that I care about, and my parents have grown to accept that. I've always been a strong writer, so my parents might be surprised if I got a C in English, but besides that they expect that I won't do well in my other classes. I've told my parents many times that through my eating disorder I have lost the ability to care about the small things in life that don't really matter. Writing matters to me and I spend hours at home every day writing poems and essays about my views of myself and life itself.

I have had a second chance many times in my life, and I realize that there are emotional problems that I have to get over before I can focus all my attention on school. Truly I am trying, trying to keep my mind together so I don't break down, and for me that is enough. I am going to go to another year of private school after high school, and hopefully by then I will be able to bring my grades up.

Chapter 4
JUNIOR HIGH:
Maintain Interest While Dealing with the Social Scene

GENERAL GUIDELINES

51.

The best thing, academically, that you can do for your junior-high children is, still, to keep them reading and writing on their own, while nourishing any academic or artistic interests they have.

Even if your children are doing all of their homework, the amount of reading and writing assigned won't be enough to ensure a really high degree of literacy (and high test scores). So find magazines and books they like, and encourage them to do personal and creative writing. (You might also check my earlier books for more suggestions.)

Nor will they probably receive the level of science or math or history or fine-arts instruction to support a real talent in one of these areas. So do what you can with books and special courses and instructors. You want to keep their enthusiasm alive. Also, a high degree of expertise in one area often spills over and sparks an interest in others.

Sophisticated reading and writing skills and a passionate academic interest will carry them much farther than high junior-high grades.

52.

Resign yourself to the fact that junior high is often the low point for homework completion.

A large percentage of my students tell me this. Homework in elementary school was easy for them, and they got a chance to do much of it in school. But then junior high comes along, they get much less independent working time, and they have many different teachers all giving homework.

So a lot of kids simply bow out of the homework scene. Or do some of the homework but somehow never get it from their lockers to the teacher's desk. Or do a hasty, incomplete version on the bus on the way to school.

Again, if your kids are doing well on the tests and on in-school assignments, and are still reading and showing academic interests on their own, I wouldn't worry too much. Let the natural consequences (low grades, having to stay after school, etc.) happen, but don't add your own punishments on top of it.

53.

Also resign yourself to the fact that social issues will often crowd out homework for junior-high kids.

When my youngest daughter was in junior high, she came home one day and said matter-of-factly, "Well, Erin was kicked out of the popular group today."

"How was she kicked out?" I asked, puzzled. I had the fuzzy, adult idea that you make and lose friends gradually.

"Well," Molly explained, "they picked up her tray off of the popular lunch table and told her she had to sit somewhere else. So she sat with us."

"So you're not in the popular group?" I guessed.

"No, I'm in the middle group. We're not the most popular, but we're not the losers, either."

This exchange shook me up—it all

seemed so ruthless somehow—but it did help explain my daughter's new worry about status, her insistence on having the "right" clothes, and her seeming need to spend hours every night on the phone hashing these issues out with her friends. And all of these preoccupations, of course, cut deeply into homework time.

54.

You also need to accept the fact that junior-high teachers will not know your children as well, or be as willing to treat them individually, as their elementary-school teachers did.

Junior-high teachers see between a hundred and a hundred and fifty students a day. And in most cases they see kids for only forty-five minutes each day, instead of all day.

This means they are not usually as flexible as elementary-school teachers. Nor are they as likely to call home at the first sign of trouble. For some students this means they aren't as motivated to work, since they are used to working for a teacher who is more personally interested in them. For other kids, this distance from the teacher gives

them a heady sense of freedom, and they take advantage of it to slack off.

While this change in teacher involvement is difficult for some parents and students to deal with, I think it's good in the long run. It pushes kids out of the nest, so to speak, and helps them get ready for the much greater independence of high school and college.

55.

Grades matter only a little in junior high; it's still really skill and knowledge that count the most.

Junior-high grades are only important as far as ensuring a good high-school placement. A selective high school will look at grades for admittance decisions, and a public high school will look at them for class placement. But even here, high standardized test scores trump grades. Most schools with restricted admission I know about have a sliding scale, where lower grades are okay if the student has high test scores. Private schools are usually delighted to get kids with high standardized scores, no matter what the grades, and public schools, although they might initially place a student in a lower level, will move him up when it becomes obvious how bright and skilled he is.

Sophisticated literacy skills, an interest in learning, and a habit of working are becoming more important all the time. These are the underlying abilities that will enable your children to do well at the highest, most demanding level of study. So keep your kids reading and nurture their academic interests.

56.

With all this said, it is still good if they can get into the habit of doing all of their homework assignments.

Then they are better prepared for high school, where grades *do* matter. Also, as course work gets harder, it becomes more difficult for even bright kids to keep up if they routinely skip assignments. Doing homework also develops self-discipline.

I think it's hard for us adults to understand sometimes how kids can just skip assignments. But if we consider how casual we are about following good eating guidelines, or exercising, or giving up bad habits like smoking or eating chocolate, it becomes easier to understand how our young teenage children have such difficulty turning their backs on fascinating telephone conversations in order to memorize boring vocabulary words.

MAKING IT MORE LIKELY YOUNG TEENAGERS DO HOMEWORK

57.

Take an even more casual interest in their work than you did when they were in elementary school.

Most elementary schools give pretty regular feedback to parents, with conferences and work sent home, so even if parents are following my advice and showing a friendly, supportive, but casual interest, they probably have a good idea of what's going on. That changes in junior high, and some parents react by regularly calling all of the teachers and asking for updates.

Avoid doing this kind of thing. Kids hate having parents do it—trust me on this one—and the anger they feel may spill over and make them disinclined to do work they would have done otherwise.

Even if you got away with this kind of

close surveillance in grade school, you probably won't in junior high, and you certainly won't in high school. So stop right now. There's no future in it. Kids *must* learn to be responsible for their own work, and they won't if you are hanging over their shoulder, and bugging their teachers.

58. *Especially avoid trying to organize your kids.*

Teachers are always quick to complain that students aren't *organized* enough. This usually means that kids fail to write down all of their assignments, have a backpack full of crumpled papers and ripped notebooks, and wait until the last minute to do long-term projects. This becomes especially noticeable in junior high since, with all of the different teachers and classes, they have more to keep track of.

A simple thing you can do is to be as generous as you can about getting them whatever kind of backpacks and notebooks and pen holders they want. Offer to replace them frequently. The novelty of having fresh, unsmudged stuff might motivate them to take a little more care with their things.

But I think the main problem with these kids is that they aren't very invested in their schoolwork, and so just don't bother keeping up with it. Trying to organize them will have the opposite effect, since your becoming involved gives them even less reason to make the effort on their own. So just refuse to do it.

My own children tended to be "unorganized" (really disinterested) during various times in their school careers, but now all three of them put me to shame as far as organizing their work—because now they are doing things they really care about.

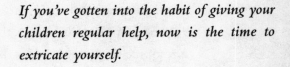

59. *If you've gotten into the habit of giving your children regular help, now is the time to extricate yourself.*

It's really easy to slide into doing this, and for some children and parents it worked fairly well in elementary school. But this kind of nightly tutoring will work less and less well as your children progress into secondary school. They simply aren't working as hard as they should if you're sitting next to them helping them along the way, and pretty soon they will resent your help as well. The rule of thumb is: The more you do, the less they do.

So stop. If your child truly needs serious academic help, the school should be providing it now in the form of tutors and special classes. You can't continue to provide this help indefinitely. Few parents have the time, for one thing, and the last thing a parent/teen relationship needs is the stress of nightly homework sessions together. Stop!

60.

But occasional help is fine, as long as it is at your children's request.

Giving occasional help, at their specific request, simply puts you in the category of a resource they use. It keeps them in control of the homework. Just remember to give only the help requested.

My children used to occasionally ask me to proofread English papers for them. The difficulty, for me, was in just proofreading. I could see all kinds of ways they could make the paper better. But I didn't volunteer my ideas, because I was afraid that then they would lose the self-confidence and sense of accomplishment they had gotten from writing the paper. Better to let their teacher make the suggestions, if she was so inclined, since kids *expect* English teachers to make suggestions.

You need to keep your long-term goals firmly in mind. Children who are enthusiastic about working will, sooner or later, do much better work than kids who just grind out assignments because someone is standing over them.

How Problems Snowball

How a basically good, hardworking kid can get in trouble with homework. (He's now doing fine.)

In elementary school I did a lot of homework. I always got good grades. My parents got divorced when I was five or six, and I was living with my mother then. My stepfather came into the picture in fifth or sixth grade. We didn't get along and I ended up moving out in seventh grade. I lived with my father all through junior high. My father remarried but that was fine; I liked her. There was a more relaxed atmosphere at my father's. They left homework up to me. But I did fine. I never really didn't do my homework.

Halfway through eighth grade my father moved to Concord. I was with him through freshman and sophomore year. I always did fine. I made honor roll freshman year. I was much happier. I remember being miserable in elementary school, staying up in my room doing homework. In high school I was also playing sports, and that had a lot to do with it.

Junior year my mom divorced my stepfather and moved to Concord. I moved back with her, which was a lot harder than I thought it would be. I was a lot different when I moved back. Plus I left a little brother and sister back with my father, and I was really attached to them.

Junior year started off about the same as other years. I was playing football, but then I got in trouble and I got kicked off the team. That started a downward spiral. Everyone was disappointed and I was more than everyone. It happened quickly. I just stopped caring, totally. I stopped doing assignments. When I didn't feel like doing them, I wouldn't go to class that day. That continued throughout junior year. I thought I would play lacrosse in the spring, but in a few weeks I got a letter saying I was ineligible and I said forget it. I figured it was because of the football thing. I couldn't deal with it. Three weeks after the season started, the athletic director came up and said the letter was a mistake. Then I started hating the school and the administration. I had talked to people and it was like I was talking to a brick wall, no matter what I said. I was also really sick but no one believed me. They assumed I was smoking marijuana. But I really was sick and I couldn't run. I had a patch of pneumonia and from that I got exercise-induced asthma. Whenever I would try to run, I could only run for three minutes.

Then toward the end of junior year I realized the trouble I put myself in. So senior year I started playing football again and was having a much better year. I was on academic probation, but it was probably good because I couldn't skip or anything. Last year it started with everyone talking about how important junior year was, then getting kicked off and everyone telling me how disappointed they were. It was basically my mom. Finally I told her I was playing for myself, not for her. I just liked playing. Parents should stay interested but not try to control. That just made me angry and made me not want to do it.

61.

Encourage them to express their opinions about their assignments and teachers.

You do this to keep them talking with you, to validate their opinions, and to allow an outlet for the angry feelings some of the assignments may be causing. Angry feelings don't go away when kept inside; they just become toxic.

So encourage your children to talk about their classes and teachers. Even if you don't agree with their assessments, say something supportive like, "Well, yes, I can see how you could feel that." If they are having a hard time, be sympathetic: "It must be really difficult for you to walk into that class every day."

Allowing them to express their frustrations isn't a magic bullet that will make problems go away, but I think you'll be surprised at how much it helps. I've had students, and my own children, rave to me about how angry they were over a situation, and then go gamely back in and deal with it. Of course, I'm then frantic with worry, upset, ready to call the marines—and they're *fine*.

62.

Do what you can to help your kids feel comfortable socially.

You don't want your children to be unhappy, because they're your *children* and you love them. But the homework reason for helping them out here is that sadness and depression can make kids stop functioning well in all areas of their lives.

So—if you possibly can—buy those name-brand clothes for them, let them talk on the phone, and allow them to go to the movies and get pizza with their friends. You don't want them to feel isolated and different. If you've maintained fairly strict rules for them when they were younger—about television watching, the kinds of foods they eat, who they play with—now is the time to loosen up. Junior-high kids like to do what the crowd is doing. Later, in high school and college, teenagers become more independent and happily go their own way. But not now.

If your children see you as a parent who is supportive, they'll be more likely to confide in you about social issues. Then you can give gentle social guidance that has a chance of being accepted.

63.

Encourage their participation in other activities, as long as the activities don't crowd out schoolwork.

I think it's important by junior high to encourage children to play a sport, or try out for drama productions, or play in the school band, or write for the newspaper. Something! Being part of an activity goes a long way toward easing the kind of friendship and young-love problems that can be so overwhelming for kids.

I think this kind of participation also helps kids learn to budget their time. Just be sure that you support whatever activities they choose. Kids are all different, and just because your older daughter loved soccer doesn't mean your son has to also. Maybe he's a natural-born trombone player.

And remember that success in any outside activity will spill over and make them feel better about life in general—and maybe homework in particular.

PROBLEMS WITH CLASSES
AND ASSIGNMENTS

64.

When simply expressing their frustration to you isn't enough to get your kids working again, ask if they would like you to intervene.

I've been teaching for almost thirty years and have seen a number of junior-high and high-school teachers who simply shouldn't be anywhere near a classroom. I don't think this problem is quite as common in elementary school, since a really bad teacher has more trouble surviving the parental outrage generated by their children spending a whole day, every day, with this teacher. But in secondary school, kids are there for only one period a day, and kids *hate* having their parents call, and administrators hate having to deal with firings . . . and bad situations drag on for years and years.

65.

If your children say no to your intervention, then—barring a really awful situation—respect their request.

I realized long ago that, in most cases, a bad decision children make is less harmful than a good decision that adults make and impose on them. If your child is in real danger of serious harm, then, of course, you have to act. But if your child is just uncomfortable, and getting lousy grades, then I wouldn't intervene without the child's okay.

Look at it this way. Suppose it's your daughter and she dislikes her science teacher because he gives boys all of the attention and respect. That's a very frustrating experience for her, but if you call him up against her wishes, then you have also treated her as someone whose wishes are not worthy of respect. What's the lesson there? I think it's better for you to listen and support her at home. This gives her the confidence eventually to stand up to that teacher herself in school.

By junior high, you'll only have your children home for five or six more years. They *have* to become independent soon.

66.

If your children want you to intervene, do so, but in as tactful a way as possible.

Basically, you're going to let them call the shots here. Give them some options. Should you request a conference, call the teacher, call the principal . . . what? Conventional wisdom says it's better to start with the teacher, but some teachers simply are not reasonable, and your children know the lay of the land better than you. Plus you're helping to rebuild their self-confidence by letting them take the lead. If your child says to go right to the principal, that's what I'd do.

I had this kind of situation when my son was in seventh grade. He had a terrible math teacher. I called the principal and said, "I don't care how you do it, but I want him out of that class. Move him up a level, move him down a level, change his whole schedule around, but move him out." The principal told me that if he moved every kid out of that teacher's class whose parent requested it, the class would be empty. (Yes! He really said that.) But when the principal realized how adamant I was, he moved him up a level to a much better teacher.

67.

Even if your child doesn't want you to intervene, do it anyway if the teacher seems to be emotionally abusive.

I think that's the kind of situation you just can't tolerate, and your child may be afraid to give you the go-ahead. He's afraid that if a change is requested and he *isn't* transferred to another class, the teacher will retaliate.

I don't think this situation happens very often, but if it does, you need to call the principal—or the superintendent, or the school committee—and insist that your child be moved. If there is simply no other class to put him in, have him placed in a study hall. He can take the course in summer school.

Terrified children aren't more likely to do homework; they are more likely to retreat into depression and do no work at all.

68.

If the teacher is generally fine but the assignments are tedious and nonmotivating, let your child handle the situation.

The thing is, life is full of these kind of situations, from high school to college to the workplace. You won't always be around to intervene, so let your child start handling the problem now.

Generally when this is the case kids either do a quick and cursory job or ignore the assignments altogether. Only very conscientious children do a thorough job on boring assignments—and being so conscientious can carry its own risks.

I think the worst thing to do is to tell your child that he's wrong, that the assignment is really interesting and you can't understand why he won't do it. You won't change your child's mind; you'll just make him furious.

PROBLEMS WITH YOUR CHILD'S ABILITY TO DO THE WORK

69.

Take very seriously the problems of children floundering with the academic requirements of junior high.

The stakes become higher in junior high, because most junior highs have kids in leveled classes. This means that if your daughter is doing poorly in math, she'll be placed in a low-level math class. Not only will this put her permanently behind, it will throw her in with a group of kids who probably don't care very much about schoolwork. And, with peer pressure being what it is at this age, she may also start to think schoolwork isn't worth bothering with.

A low-level English or history class isn't quite as bad, since those are subjects that aren't so hierarchical. Placement in a low-level seventh-grade English class doesn't mean placement in a low-level class forever—as it probably does in math. But even so, you want to avoid having your children in these classes altogether, if you can.

So what do you do if you have a child who simply can't seem to do junior-high work?

70. Try hard to get your low-achieving child to talk with you about the school difficulty.

Let's say it's your daughter. Sit down with her and try to figure out exactly what subjects are causing the problem. And what exactly the problem is. Is there too much material for her to remember in history? Is the reading too hard for her in English? What part of math is too difficult for her?

What you're trying to do is get a sense of whether the problem is really academic or if it's something else. I think in elementary school parents need to be the detectives, but by junior high the kids themselves usually have the best sense of what's going on, although they may have trouble articulating it.

A Work Ethic
and Love of Reading

This interview is with an African American young man who has done so well in high school that he was accepted early to Brown University. Notice, though, that he's the oldest child, and reports that his parents are having a harder time instilling this work ethic in his younger brothers.

My dad grew up on Long Island in New York. His father was a Pullman porter on the railroad. They weren't a rich family; they were rather poor. My dad was driven in part to get out of that situation. He knows what it's like to come from a family that didn't have the opportunities. He's a doctor who went to MIT. He looks back on where he was as a child and where he is now, and says it shows what hard work can do for you. He knows you need to work hard to do well. Families that don't have that experience or don't know about that firsthand can't really instill that sort of drive in someone.

My mother came from a family of six kids. Her father was in the army during WWII. She was the second oldest, so she had to help take care of six kids. I guess her family lived in Connecticut, a rural area. She learned how to drive working on a farm, driving a tractor. The whole family worked on the farm. My grandmother taught languages. There was a whole lot of drive to do well in that family, too.

I was always pressured to do well. It was always, "You have to do as well as you can. That way you can do better in life. You can break the stereotype."

I started reading a lot in first or second grade in Michigan. At the time I was really interested in trains because my dad had a model set in the basement that he built. So I'd read books on trains and the engineers. The love of history was due to my fourth-grade teacher. He was a history nut and I got hooked. Some things are hard—I don't memorize math or science easily, but history—facts and dates and time periods—those stick. It also helps having a broad background on the subject.

Middle school was interesting. I loved English, to have a class where I had to read. I got the Bookworm Award in sixth grade. I sometimes slacked in math because I really didn't like it. It was bad. I kick myself looking back at it. Why did I do that? My parents got on my case a lot about math homework. "You'll be on the street, you won't be able to get a job. . . ." I did get a math tutor and it got better.

I'm a very literal person and I find it hard to analyze a story. When we did *Their Eyes Were Watching God,* my mom read some of it because I really had no idea what I was writing about. She read the book and really liked it. That's always helpful. Some parents don't have time to do that, to give someone the feeling that they're not on their own in this, that they can ask for help, that their parents are there. They didn't impose. But if I had a question, I could always ask. If they didn't know, they didn't, but they'd help me if they could.

You need a good relationship with your parents. I have two brothers and a sister. I'm the oldest. My sister is like me; she's driven. My nine-year-old brother cares more about playing, and so he and my other brother don't have the same drive. It baffles me as to why. My mom's frustrated and so is my dad. I think my brother is the type of person who doesn't react well to authority. And I don't know. I really don't know.

71.

Believe what your young teens tell you about the reasons for their failure.

Sometimes, as parents, we are inclined to dismiss a real problem. If your daughter tells you that she can't concentrate in class, or while studying at home, work with her to find out the reason. Is she overtired? Sleeping all right? Eating enough? Is she worried about something?

Sometimes family disruptions (divorce, death, a move) cause kids to stop working. I think it's very hard for us as parents to face the reality that family troubles or changes can have such global consequences in our children's lives. Often we can't do anything about the situation except say, "I'm so sorry, honey, and I wish I could make things better for you. Tell me what I can do to help." I don't think it ever helps to belittle a child's concern, saying something like, "You're just making too big a deal about this." Even if you privately think that, don't *say* it.

And I'm a big believer in professional help, although you may have to look around a bit to find just the right person.

72.

If the problem really seems to be just academic, ask the school to do testing for learning disabilities.

Although a serious learning problem should have been picked up in elementary school, I think some kids with learning disabilities are so bright, they manage to slide through undetected until junior high or even high school. So even if your child has had a very successful school experience up to now, don't be afraid to ask for educational testing. Just knowing what the problem is can go a long way toward solving it.

I was tested in high school and found to be in the two percentile for visual memory, which means that ninety-eight percent of the population tested better than I did. I was amazed! And *relieved* finally to understand why I failed every map test, and spelling test, I ever took. I simply can't hold a visual picture in my mind. But once I knew the problem, I could figure out ways of compensating.

73.

If a disability is found, and is severe enough to warrant an Individual Education Plan, make sure your child agrees with the help mandated in the plan.

While elementary-school kids seem to slide off to a resource room without too much of a problem, junior-high kids can be very resistant. And while I know this goes against conventional wisdom, I wouldn't force them. Because what's the point? If you have to force them, the chance of them getting much out of the tutoring is pretty remote—and chances are you've kicked up all kinds of hostile feelings toward you and toward school.

No, explain the options and let your child make the final call. I find that kids who have parents who are supportive but not intrusive are usually able to take advantage of extra help. If they don't want the help, it may be because they have reason to know it's not very good—or they just feel that their social status is too shaky to withstand being labeled a "sped" kid. Whatever their reasons, you have to respect them.

74.

If the academic problems are major, and your child refuses special ed help, consider private tutors.

Because private tutoring takes place out of school, and because you can select a private tutor who's really good, it's sometimes more acceptable to the kid who'd rather die than be seen hanging out in a special ed resource room. And, with a tutor, you avoid the tensions that arise when a parent tries to do the tutoring.

I think the best way to find one is to ask around. The guidance department of your child's school may have some suggestions, or check with other parents. If you can't find anyone that way, you could advertise in a local paper and then interview the promising candidates. In hiring, I think I'd go for personal qualities over an academic résumé. You want someone who can excite your child about learning—not make him feel even dumber.

75.

As a last resort, consider changing schools.

I would really only do this as a last resort because, again, social issues are so paramount for this age group, and changing schools can be traumatic. But, on the other hand, kids who are failing in school often have social problems as well, so a change could help on all fronts.

Look around really carefully before making a change. If you're checking out private schools, look for one that goes through high school, as the last thing you want is to have to make another change in two years. If you're thinking of moving to get access to a different public school system, be sure you visit the school. Don't go just on reputation and standardized scores. Look for a school system that has a culture your child can be comfortable in.

Chapter 5
HIGH SCHOOL

GENERAL GUIDELINES

76.

In high school, sophisticated reading skills and independent academic interests are still more important than grades.

This is because these abilities stay with your kids, and make it possible for them to do advanced work in college. Kids who get high grades but don't read very well—or don't have a habit of independent work—will "ceiling-out" soon. They may get in a good college but probably won't be able to stay there. Kids with low grades but excellent abilities may not get into the best universities right away but will probably get into very good ones (with their high SAT scores), and can always transfer later to better colleges, if they wish.

Skills and a love of learning: That's what will serve your kids well over the long haul.

77.

But, realistically, grades (and homework) do count in high school.

By high school, grades and homework are inextricably linked. Kids who do no work outside of class—unless they are in a very low track—won't pass their courses, or will pass with a very low grade. They can't pass their English classes, for example, without reading the books and writing the papers. And failing English means they won't graduate.

And, of course, grades count for college acceptance.

78.

Grade pressure from parents, however, becomes even more counterproductive in high school.

Some of my students use the term "Mom Résumé" (originated by a teacher at my school, Nikki Willis), as in "My mother wants me to get into Harvard for her Mom Résumé," or "My older brother was such a screw-up that I'm the last chance for her Mom Résumé."

If your daughter is saying this: not good. Lay off; you're alienating her with your expectations. And few kids who are angry and alienated do their best work.

And, again, too much grade pressure from parents can result in wide-scale cheating, a really bad thing to have happen.

79.

A warm, friendly interest, however, is still critical.

Teenagers are so insecure. You need to keep *telling* them how smart they are, how handsome, how engaging and mature. How proud you are of them for their hard work in school . . . and what, exactly, *are* they doing in school now?

Teenagers who feel loved and cherished are much more likely to think they deserve good grades—and therefore be willing to work for them. It's a hard line to walk between not showing any interest (and so making them think you don't care) and showing too much (and making them think you only love them for their achievements). But I think an interest that is always focused on your kids themselves, rather than on their achievements, pays off the best in the long run. I wouldn't say: "I can't believe you're getting such lousy grades. We've got to do something to bring those grades up!" I would say, however: "I'm really worried about you. How can I help you start to do better?"

80.

A studious peer group is a huge support and incentive for high-school kids to do well in school.

While you can't choose the friends your high-school kids make, you can make it more likely that they'll choose kids interested in academic achievement if you keep a few things in mind. One is that most participants in school activities are usually good students. So encourage an interest in school clubs or sports. I know conventional wisdom says that high-school "jocks" are dumb, but that's not the case. Usually athletes work very hard in class, as well as on the field. And kids who write for the school newspaper or yearbook, or participate in student government, are usually among the best students.

And don't judge your children's friends by their looks. As I write this, one of my best students has blue hair, and one of my other best students walks around with chains around her waist, jingling cheerfully, their silver shine showing off her all-black outfits.

The Perils of Pressuring Kids

I asked to interview this student after I caught him cheating in my class. It turned out he had cheated his way all through high school. His parents insisted on good grades; he found the easiest way of obliging them.

There wasn't really homework until fifth grade. It was pretty easy. My parents have another room for me without a phone or television where I can't actually do anything else . . . except when I'm in there, I usually find something else to do instead of the homework.

Middle school was a lot easier than fifth grade. Still, I did a half-assed job just to get it done. With math problems I'd just put a question mark next to the problem to show I looked at it. With reading assignments I'd sometimes read or skim it. I'd know in advance when there'd be a quiz, so I could go over it. I'd ask my friends. It was kind of a collaboration. I didn't use Cliff Notes. Movies, yes. I have a philosophy: It's not a good book if it doesn't have a movie.

In high school it got really tough and I'd depend on my friends. I'd do a little and a friend would and we'd just copy each other's to make it faster so I could go outside. First year I played a lot of sports and I didn't have time to do anything. My grades started to fall and my parents got me a tutor and I got the tutor to do all my homework so they'd keep paying her and she'd keep coming. My grades went up with the tutor, but it wasn't my work, it was the tutor's. She would rewrite stuff for me and I'd just have to type it up.

Sophomore year I dropped a few sports. It was more of the same. I'd copy off friends and they'd copy off me, skim the reading, just get an easy way out of it, however that may be. In high school it's a lot easier because a lot of different classes meet on different days. You could ask someone in the same section. High school was a lot easier to bullshit your way through.

If I wasn't on honor roll every term, I'd be in trouble. My parents made sure I had my homework done before I could go out. They'd time me, tell me two hours was minimal. But if I'm on honor roll, they assume I'm getting stuff done. Otherwise they stress the amount of time and effort I should put into it. That was a big motivation to keep grades up. Just get it done, get the grades. I don't think my parents emphasized learning, it was just good grades to get in a good college. They just assumed with good grades I was learning a lot.

My advice for parents is not to pressure your kids because that will make them too worried that they have to succeed. That just makes kids go down the wrong direction, do anything possible just to get stuff done.

81.

It's also important to help free them up from chores and work, as much as you can, so they have time to study.

Many parents I know require that their high-school children earn all of their own spending money, and start saving a considerable amount for college. If both parents are working flat-out, and money is very tight, that's a reasonable request. But I don't understand families who have a bit more money—and perhaps even have one parent who isn't working at all—requiring this of their children.

Working long hours always hurts kids' ability to study, especially if the ki~ playing sports as well. They si~ have the time and energy ~ seven hours a day, ~ another two or th~ of homewor~ all of th~ atte~

s~ hav~

112

Mary Leonhardt

So if you are serious about your children doing well in school, you need to put your money where your mouth is, so to speak. Give them some spending money. Don't tie them up for hours with household chores. Let them know that their doing well in school is a real priority for you, a priority that you're willing to make sacrifices for.

82. *The other reason for discouraging employment is that kids who have a lot of money in high school don't find studying and the thought of college as compelling.*

Hey, they think they're doing pretty well right now: a big stereo, maybe a cool car, plenty of money for partying. They don't realize that the two hundred bucks a week they're making won't go far when they're paying rent, buying food, and supporting a family.

Also, realistically, most college kids exist on a pretty tight budget. It's good to get them used to that now so they won't be distracted from college studying by money worries—and so they'll be used to the "study hard, spend little" lifestyle of successful college kids.

CHOOSING CLASSES

83.

In high school, students usually get more of a choice about classes. Don't push them to take advanced classes unless they want to themselves.

This is very hard. *We* know our children are very bright. Why don't *they,* or the school, recognize that fact?

The problem is that even if you have a child with the ability to be in an advanced class, unless motivation and a willingness to work hard are coupled with the ability, disaster will result. High-school teachers are even less willing than junior-high ones to nudge a reluctant kid along through an honors or advanced-placement course. In the movies a teacher can get the most reluctant learners to become proficient in advanced calculus. In real life that teacher probably has a student load of a hundred and fifty kids and barely enough time during the day even to go to the bathroom. Rarely does a publi high-school teacher have the time per ally to tutor a reluctant student through an entire semester or year of work.

So don't set your child up for failure.

84.

But do all you can to make it possible for your kids to take advanced classes if they want to themselves.

I used to, at my son's request, routinely override the school's recommendation for his math placement. Tim always wanted to be in a higher level than the school thought he should be. It turned out well, too: He ended up minoring in math in college, and is now a financial analyst for a large company in Boston. But I used to have to sign these sheets saying that I understood I was going against the math department's recommendation, and I understood he would get no more extra help than any other student.

Tim, as it turned out, never needed any extra tutoring to do higher-level math, but if he had, I would have found a tutor for him—because he *wanted* to do the math. That's everything.

85.

Let your children choose their own elective courses.

By eleventh grade, electives are usually a large part of students' schedules. In the school I teach at, for example, freshman and sophomore English are required courses, but the students get to choose from a variety of junior and senior English electives. The same thing is true in social studies and, to a lesser extent, in foreign language, music, and art.

It's tempting to insist that kids take the courses that will look the best on their college applications, but I would caution against that. Interest is everything in motivating students to work hard. Plus, just the fact that they chose the course themselves makes them much more inclined to invest time and energy in it.

And, realistically, a high grade and an enthusiastic teacher recommendation from a course in sports psychology will carry them farther than a mediocre grade and recommendation from an economics teacher—never mind the fact that they'll have learned more, too, in the bargain.

86.

Somehow, make sure they have access to a computer.

By high school, I think this is really necessary. Most high schools now have computer labs, and if your children have enough study periods, or are able to stay after school to work, the school lab may be enough. If not, you need to get a computer they can use at home.

By now they should be doing all of their papers on the computer. I doubt if any college professors accept handwritten essays these days, and fewer and fewer high-school teachers do. Also, the Internet is a wonderful academic resource. Not only can they check out library holdings on-line, they can download many articles and news stories right away.

The students who are best with computers, I've found, are the ones who have a computer at home, and a knowledgeable parent or sibling who will help them. Schools are so nervous about security and lawsuits that it's very hard for kids to do the kind of playing around with computers at school that gives them really sophisticated skills.

But somewhere, at school or at home, your kids have to start being comfortable using a computer.

87.

Don't overlook the little things you can do to help.

Bringing a cup of hot chocolate to a teenager studying late, letting your daughter drive your car to school so she doesn't waste time waiting for the school bus, keeping younger siblings quiet when your son has a big test the next day—all of these little things convey the message that academics are important, and that you appreciate the effort your kids are putting into their schoolwork.

With teenagers, believe me, this kind of gentle, thoughtful support goes much, much farther than pressure and punishments (which don't work at all).

ROADBLOCKS TO HIGH-SCHOOL SUCCESS

88.

Worries about social acceptance can still have a global effect on ability to work well.

My sense is that many kids who had such a difficult time in junior high do better by high school. There seem to be more social groups they can join; moreover, classmates are a little more tolerant. If your children have found a few friends who seem supportive and kind, be thankful—even if the friends look a little strange to you.

But if you have a child who seems very much alone, I'd start thinking about some professional help. A therapist can be very effective in coaching kids how to navigate the social scene.

89.

An abrupt drop-off in work can signal a drug or alcohol problem.

We don't like to think about it, but drugs and alcohol are a huge part of the high-school social scene. The great majority of kids I know seem to be able to try these for-

bidden substances but not get addicted. They're occasional party users.

We don't like this, naturally, but I don't know any effective way of preventing it. Prohibiting your children from attending parties might work (although I've had enough kids describe to me how they sneak out of their houses that I'm doubtful), but even if it does, what's going to happen when they go away to college? Party City, that's what's going to happen, and you won't be there to help bail them out of trouble.

No, the only thing that works, I'm sure, is to have a strong enough relationship with your children that they'll still talk with you and trust you. They won't tell you everything (they're *teenagers*), but if they feel valued and loved and trusted, they'll have strong reasons for staying out of major trouble. And if they do get in over their heads, they'll accept help.

90. *Depression, or eating disorders, or anxiety problems can also cause a drop in work.*

In my twenty-nine years of teaching, I've had around ten or twelve students make suicide attempts—none successful, thank God.

I've had many more on medication or in therapy. I don't know if more kids are depressed or anxious now than when I started teaching, or if we're just more alert about picking up on these conditions, but they're there. Trust me, they're there.

So watch for them. If your daughter used to be a terrific student but now mopes around the house, refusing to read books or start papers, take her to a therapist for an evaluation. As mental health professionals keep telling us, depression is a treatable condition. I'm not a therapist, only a teacher, but my own observation is that kids who become promiscuous, or rebellious, or withdrawn, should be evaluated, as should kids who can't seem to get work done because they're perfectionists. Therapy and/or medication really do help. They save lives.

When You Have a Really Creative Child

This interview is with a sophomore of mine, Amelia Atwater-Rhodes, who has been a published author since the age of thirteen. Now, at fifteen, her first book, In the Forests of the Night, *is doing very well, and she has a second book coming out this spring, as well as a contract for a third book. But because life is never perfect, one of the costs of this degree of creativity is a reluctance—almost an inability—to keep up with regular old boring high-school homework.*

I started writing after fifth grade, that summer. I started writing because I'm a really fast reader and I finish books really quickly and so I started writing my own books to occupy some time. There's not that much to do in Concord. With me, writing has a priority. If there's something I want to write, nothing can drag me from my computer. So far I've written twenty-five books—I really enjoy writing, just meeting the characters.

We didn't really have homework until fourth or fifth grade. The whole workload wasn't that great at first. School has always been pretty easy for me—I can usually listen in class and do well on tests without ever doing homework or studying. I am presently a sophomore in high school, and this is the first year that I am having trouble at school, mainly due to forgetting or simply ignoring homework. Sometimes I'll sit down to do homework and I'll do it for a while. But I get bored quickly unless someone is with me; even if that person is just my mother, cooking nearby, my homework gets finished—unusual in itself—better and faster than it would if I was alone.

My mom has always been very loose about it. "Try your best," she says, but she hasn't ever said that if I don't do all my homework, she's going to ground me. The worst thing my mom does is look disappointed. It's my mom who brings me back and says, "Amy, there are other things you need to be doing." They don't want me to lose the other skills. If I flunk math, for example, that would also drag me down to a lower science. They don't want me to cut off my options now.

Sometimes I can incorporate my schoolwork into writing, like in history. I have lots of historical characters. When we're learning about the time frames, I'll do extra reading just because it interests me. When you compare that to fifty math questions, all of which do the same thing . . . It's hard to get motivated for something that doesn't interest me. I'm very motivated about what I want to do. I'm interested in just about everything, but I have problems in chemistry because I'm not keeping up with math.

I never put my name on anything I don't feel strongly about. I enjoy writing. The main thing about my family is, brilliance runs through it. My sister is the straight-A-no-effort student. Yeah, it's a hard act to follow. First semester of her in college and I'm looking forward to seeing B's on her report card. But it was all A's.

91.

If your children are showing these problems, get them help, while being very clear that your main priority is their health and well-being, not their grades.

A good first place to look for help is your family doctor, although some HMOs, I know, let you bypass regular referral procedures and directly make an appointment for a mental health evaluation. And virtually all HMOs and insurance companies now pay for some kind of treatment.

It's also important to know that, with these kinds of problems, you may have to suspend for a while your rule that your child calls the shots on whether or not to get help. The nature of depression and addiction makes it very hard for kids to realize their need for therapy. If you've been very respectful of your children's autonomy and abilities up to now, your relationship should weather this necessary intrusion on your part. And, of course, try to help them make the decision themselves first. But if they absolutely refuse, and if the situation is serious enough, insist on the help. If your kids know it's done out of love for them, it should be okay.

The good news is that when these conditions are under control, schoolwork almost always takes an upswing.

COLLEGE IN MIND

92. *Don't make the mistake of letting your children think that only a handful of colleges will be acceptable to you.*

I've had students tell me that their parents say they *must* get into an Ivy League college. Or into the parents' alma mater. Or into one highly rated by *U.S. News & World Report*. It's hard to know what parents are thinking of when they make these pronouncements, because all the results I see are negative. Kids under this kind of pressure rarely do the best work, no matter how hard they try. And if they're tired of this kind of stress—and seriously annoyed at their parents—they may stop trying altogether.

You need to keep in mind that different colleges work well for different kids. What you're looking for is a match. You want to help your children find schools that are right for their particular academic and social needs. I had a very bright, shy teenager describe to me how she loved the junior college she was attending because the classes were so small, and the professors so approachable, that—for the first time *ever* in her school career—she was participating in class discussions, and really following what was going on. Surely that was a better place for her than a large, competitive university.

And, realistically, all that Ivy League degree gets you is an interview, or maybe a first job. After that, you're hired on what you've accomplished, not on where you've attended school. So encourage your children to find the college that will best help them develop their abilities.

93.

As your kids go off to college, encourage them to major in whatever field most interests them.

They'll do the best work in a field they love, for one thing. For another thing, do you really want your kids to work their whole lives in a field they dislike, just because it has high pay or high prestige? Life's too short for that.

Plus, I don't even think college majors are that predictive of lifelong careers. My oldest daughter majored in English and is now the head coach for a women's soccer team at a very competitive university. My son majored in European history and is a financial analyst. And my younger daughter is majoring in art. She'll probably run a horse farm or something.

Chapter 6
A FEW WORDS ABOUT GIFTED CHILDREN

94.

Don't be surprised if you have a gifted child who never seems to get around to homework.

The definition of *gifted* that has always made sense to me is Sir Arthur Conan Doyle's Sherlock Holmes quip in *A Study in Scarlet,* that "genius is an infinite capacity for taking pains." One might think this would make gifted kids good little homework-doers, but there's another phrase that should have been added: They have "an infinite capacity for taking pains" *in their area of interest.*

Their interests may change over the years, but what won't change is their single-minded pursuit of whatever is their current love. They grow into absentminded professors who invent penicillin but can't find their socks (unless, of course, you're lucky, and one of their gifts is organization).

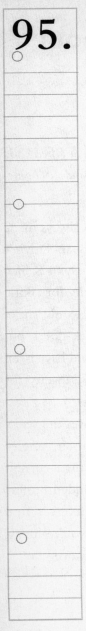

95.

Allow your gifted child to work out a system of priorities.

If you've done all of the things I've suggested, then your gifted child won't be hostile and angry with you, because you won't have nagged or punished or micromanaged. That's really good because it means that homework really may get done. It will just get done at the last minute or in a cursory manner. Conjugating Latin verbs just doesn't have priority in the life of someone who is composing an operetta.

But again, by high school, when many of these gifted kids decide they *do* want access to a top university, this other homework that they do—whenever they manage to work it in—is often beautifully done. All of their independent reading has left them with excellent reading skills, for one thing, so they can work fast, and I think a little of their passion for perfection in their interest area spills over into their other work. Not always, of course. Artists seem more single-minded about just doing art, for example, but musicians (for some reason) seem more willing to put extra effort into science, history, and English.

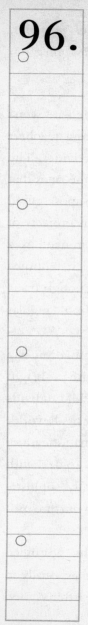

96.

It's really important to try to get gifted kids with teachers they like.

Conventional wisdom would suggest that gifted kids could do well with any teacher, but I haven't found that to be true. Certainly they could do the work in any class, but some teachers—especially those who aren't too bright, and have endless rules about notebook organization and the color of ink to use and promptness to class—drive gifted kids batty, since these kids tend not to suffer fools gladly.

If you have a quiet, compliant, gifted son, for example, who ends up with a teacher like this, he'll probably jump through all these hoops but suffer a cost in his self-esteem, feeling he's sold his soul. If your son is outspoken, on the other hand, he may end up in full-fledged war with the teacher—not a good scenario, either. Gifted girls can be hell on wheels as well.

So do what you can as far as teacher assignment.

97.

Look for flexibility in school programs, rather than for ones labeled "gifted" or "advanced."

Some programs for gifted children are wonderful, staffed by warm, exciting teachers who encourage independent activities. The programs to watch out for are the ones that just pile on extra work. Since most gifted children are already involved in projects of their own, the last thing they need is a teacher giving them more dry, "homework"-type work. They have enough trouble getting the homework from regular classes done.

Actually, I think the ideal situation is a small, heterogeneous class with a bright teacher who will give a gifted child individual attention. You have the best of all worlds there. The child is kept in the mainstream of the social scene, and learns how to deal with kids who may be more socially sophisticated—but also has a mentor to nurture special talents.

By high school, of course, advanced classes become more important, especially in areas like math or science. But I think good

heterogeneous classes in English and social studies can still work, as long as the teacher is flexible and creative about assignments.

98.

If your school district has an excellent gifted program but you can't get your child into it, don't lose any sleep over the situation.

Few (maybe none) of my really exciting, creative high-school students are products of gifted programs. Some had mentors—a teacher or parent or coach usually—and some just read and worked extensively on their own. I've had very high-achieving adults tell me that they did so well because they went to a sleepy little school that didn't give much homework, so they had plenty of time for their own work.

What most gifted kids do need is plenty of access to books and to adults willing to share their enthusiasms. Parents can fill this role as well as teachers. As kids get older, and their talents become harder for a parent to nurture (in science or music, for example), then they may need special coaches or tutors—but I think you're as likely to find them on your own as through a gifted program.

FINALLY

99.

Remember to let your children know that while schoolwork is important, it pales before the really important things in life: kindness, helpfulness, love, respect. Don't ever make the mistake of allowing your kids to think that their worth to you somehow depends on how well they do in school.

Schoolwork is, in any final reckoning, only a very small part of life.